Tough Topics

Peer Pressure

Elizabeth Raum

Heinemann Library
Chicago, Illinois

Customer Service 888-454-2279

Visit our website at www.heinemannlibrary.com

Designed by Joanna Hinton-Malivoire
Photo research by Tracy Cummins and Heather Mauldin
Printed in China by South China Printing.

12 11 10
10 9 8 7 6 5 4 3

Library of Congress Cataloging-in-Publication Data
Raum, Elizabeth.
   Peer pressure / Elizabeth Raum.
      p. cm. -- (Tough topics)
   Includes bibliographical references and index.
   ISBN-13: 978-1-4329-0821-8 (hc), ISBN-10: 1-4329-0821-9 (hc)
   ISBN 13: 978-1-4329-0826-3 (pb), ISBN-10: 1-4329-0826-X (pb)
1. Peer pressure--Juvenile literature. 2. Conformity--Juvenile literature. I. Title.
   HQ784.P43R38 2008
   303.3'27--dc22

                                 2007034114

Acknowledgments
The author and publisher are grateful to the following for permission to reproduce copyright
material: ©Coribs pp. 4 (Don Mason), 9 (zefa/Heide Benser), 13 (zefa/Emely), 26 (Hill Street/Studios/
StockThisWay); ©Getty Images pp. 5 (Simon Watson), 6 (Sean Justice), 7 (Leland Bobbe), 8 (Laurence
Moulton), 10 (Ned Frisk), 11 (Ruth Jenkinson), 12 (Stockbyte), 14, 15, 20, 24, 28, 29 (Royalty Free),
16 (Digital Vision), 17 (Lisa Peardon), 18 (Matt Henry Gunther), 21 (LWA/Dann Tardif), 22 (Camille
Tokerud), 23 (Peter Cade), 25 (Andreas Kuehn), 27 (Richard Koek).

Cover photograph reproduced with permission of ©Corbis/Thinkstock.

The author would like to thank Ms. Helen Scully, Guidance Counselor, Central Elementary School,
Warren Township, New Jersey, for her valuable assistance.

Disclaimer
All the INTERNET addresses (URLs) given in this book were valid at the time of going to press.
However, due to the dynamic nature of the internet, some addresses may have changed, or sites
may have ceased to exist since publication. While the author and publishers regret any inconvenience
this may cause readers, no responsibility for such changes can be accepted by either the author(s) or
the publishers.

Contents

Some words are shown in bold, **like this**. You can find out what they mean by looking in the Glossary.

What Is Peer Pressure?

People who are about the same age or in the same grade are called **peers**. Sometimes our peers are our friends. Children have friends, and so do adults. Everyone enjoys spending time with friends.

▲ These peers are having fun at a picnic together.

▼It can be fun to do what our peers do.

When we do things because our peers tell us to, it is called **peer pressure**. When we do things because we want to be part of a group, that's peer pressure, too. Many children do things because they want others to like them.

▲ It feels great when peers cheer for you.

Sometimes peer pressure can be good. It is fun to be part of a team or a club. Peers on sports teams may **encourage** us to practice and try harder. Peers in clubs often work together to help others.

Peers may encourage us to study harder. Peers may ask us to join a music group or take an art class. Peers who want to make the world a better place encourage us to be kind and helpful.

▲ These peers work together to help the environment.

Sometimes peer pressure is bad. It's bad when a peer puts pressure on us to do things we would not do on our own. Sometimes a peer pressures us to be unkind to others or to do things that are unsafe or **harmful**.

◄ These peers are being unkind.

▲No one wants to be left out.

Groups use peer pressure, too. Some groups leave certain children out or spread **gossip**. Groups of peers can gang up on others.

Why Do I Feel Pressured?

You may feel caught between what your peers want you to do and what you know is the right thing to do. Sometimes what your peers want to do is not bad, but it's not right for you. It's hard to say "No."

▶ It's important to think about what is right for you.

▲It's not easy to say
"No" to your peers.

Most children enjoy being part of a
group. Some children are afraid that
others will make fun of them or laugh
at them if they don't go along with the
group. It's not always easy to stand up
for yourself and do the right thing.

What Can I Do When I Feel Pressured?

The next time your peers ask you to do something, don't say "Yes" right away. Take a minute to decide what is right for you. Making a good **decision** is difficult. But you can do it.

▲Stop and think before you say "Yes."

Ask yourself: Is this something I want to do? Is this something my parents want me to do? Is it safe? Is it against the rules? Is it kind?

◀ You can make difficult decisions.

▲ These girls made a good choice to play together on the playground.

If you feel sure that what your peers want you to do is a good idea, then do it and have fun. But if it doesn't feel right, don't do it. It's better to say "No" than to go along with the group.

▼When you make good choices, you can feel proud of yourself.

Remember that you are in charge of what you do. You are a strong person with good ideas. Do what you know is best for you.

▲ If your friends make you feel left out, find new friends who will be kind to you.

It's okay if some people don't like you. It's more important to make wise choices than to be friends with everyone. Your choices make a difference in your life and the lives of others.

Tell yourself that you need friends who **respect** the choices you make. Good friends understand that sometimes you have to say "No." Good friends accept you the way you are.

▲Good friends understand your choices.

How Do I Say No?

◀ Be friendly and sure of yourself. People will know they cannot put pressure on you.

There are lots of ways to say "No." Make sure you let others know that you mean what you say. Stand up straight, smile, and say, "No."

Tell the truth. Don't be afraid to say, "My parents won't let me," or "It's against the rules." Whatever you say, make sure to say it clearly and then walk away.

How to Say No

You might say:

- No, but maybe another time.

- No way, let's do something else.

- No, I don't want to.

- No, it isn't nice.

- No, it's not safe.

- No, my parents won't let me.

Choose Friends Wisely

If your friends put too much pressure on you, make new friends. You might find new friends on a sports team. You might find new friends in your neighborhood.

▶ Choose friends who enjoy doing the things you enjoy. These children share a love of basketball.

▲ If you enjoy science, find friends who also enjoy science.

Find friends who like the things you like. If you like drawing, look for friends who like to draw. If you like swimming or biking, find friends who like these things, too.

▲ A smile tells everyone
that you are friendly.

To make a friend, smile and say, "Hi."
Look your new friend in the eyes and
invite him or her to join you in a
game or activity. Being kind shows
that you will be a good friend.

Making friends can be scary, but you'll get better and better at it. If the first person you talk to doesn't want to be your friend, don't give up. There are lots of children who would like to have you for a friend.

▲Sharing something you enjoy is a good way to begin a friendship.

◄ Good friends like spending time together.

Treat your friends the way you would like to be treated. Good friends don't put pressure on each other. Good friends respect each other's **decisions**.

◀ Good friends cheer one another up.

Good friends are kind to each other. They tell the truth and keep their promises. Good friends stick up for each other.

Talk to an Adult

You can make many **decisions** for yourself. But it's always good to talk to your parents about your decisions. Tell your parents if you are feeling pressured by a peer. They may have good ideas to help you solve the problem.

◀Parents can help.

▲Coaches can help.

Talk to your coach, your camp
counselor, or your grandparents. Your
teacher and school principal may be
able to help, too. Adults know how
hard it is to face peer pressure.

◄Teachers can help.

Sometimes peers won't take "No" for an answer. If your peers treat you badly or scare you, tell an adult right away. If your peers make you feel unsafe, tell a parent, teacher, coach, or other helpful adult.

▲School should be a safe
and happy place.

Adults need to know when there is a
problem so that they can help you.
Telling helps both you and your peers.
Telling may help other children, too.
Telling is a brave thing to do.

Glossary

decision choice

encourage help and support

gossip unkind talk about other people

harmful may cause you to hurt yourself

peer person the same age or in the same class

peer pressure when peers get you to do things you don't want to do

respect honor the ideas and beliefs of others

Find Out More

Books to Read

Brown, Laurie Krasny and Marc Brown. *How To Be A Friend.* Boston, MA: Little, Brown Young Readers, 1998.

Brumbeau, Jeff. *Miss Hunnicut's Hat.* New York: Orchard Books, 2003.

Burns, Peggy. *Playground Survival.* Chicago: Raintree, 2005.

Klingel, Cynthia Fitterer. *Friendship.* Chanhassen, MN: Child's World, 2003.

Websites

- TheCoolSpot.gov (http://www.thecoolspot.gov/pressures.asp.) is a Website that explains peer pressure.

- Kidshealth.org (www.kidshealth.org/kid) has information on health and safety topics for kids.

Index